Lent and Easter Wisdom

from

SAINT BENEDICT

D1506553

Other Books in This Series from Liguori Publications

Lent and Easter Wisdom from G.K. Chesterton

Lent and Easter Wisdom from Fulton J. Sheen

Lent and Easter Wisdom from Henri J.M. Nouwen

Lent and Easter Wisdom from Pope John Paul II

*Lent and Easter Wisdom
from Saint Francis and Saint Clare of Assisi*

Lent and Easter Wisdom from Thomas Merton

Lent and Easter Wisdom from Saint Ignatius of Loyola

ℒENT *and* ℰASTER 𝒲ISDOM

—— *from* ——

SAINT BENEDICT

Daily Scripture and Prayers Together
With Saint Benedict's Own Words

Compiled by Judith Sutera, OSB

Liguori
LIGUORI, MISSOURI

Imprimi Potest: Thomas D. Picton, CSsR
Provincial, Denver Province, The Redemptorists

Published by Liguori Publications
Liguori, Missouri
To order, call 800-325-9521
www.liguori.org

Library of Congress Cataloging-in-Publication Data

Lent and Easter wisdom from Saint Benedict : daily Scripture and prayers together with Saint Benedict's own words / compiled by Judith Sutera.—1st ed.

    p. cm.

    ISBN 978-0-7648-1968-1

1. Lent—Prayers and devotions. 2. Easter—Prayers and devotions. 3. Catholic Church—Prayers and devotions. I. Sutera, Judith. II. Benedict, Saint, Abbot of Monte Cassino. Selections. English. 2010.

    BX2170.L4L454 2010

    242'.34—dc22

                          2010024009

Printed in the United States of America
14 13 12 11 10   5 4 3 2 1
First Edition

Contents

Introduction

It is appropriate to turn to Saint Benedict and monastic wisdom in Lent, since the saint says in his rule that the monastic life should be a continuous Lent. This is not as daunting a sentiment as it might first appear to be to some readers.

To appreciate what is being suggested, one must have a broad concept of what Lent is meant to be and do. It is not merely a time of giving up pleasures and dwelling on one's sins. The giving up of pleasures is intended to make one mindful of how easy it is to fall into bad habits or indulgent behavior. The sacrifices should lead to reform and to turning back toward the healthy and holy in one's daily life. Most faith traditions also tie the sacrifice to some acts of generosity toward the needy, and certainly conscientious Christians should practice this type of activity during the rest of the year as well.

Sacrifice is also a symbolic effort at showing sorrow for one's failings and atoning for them. No one can deny that this repentance, along with making reparation for wrongs and being reconciled with others, are activities that should not be confined to a single season.

Saint Benedict, ever the realist, says that this kind of year-round attentiveness would be the ideal, but that frail humanity tends to slide away from the ideal. Benedict, in the early sixth century, was writing his summary of the monastic way of life at the end of a long period of examination of the human condition by philosophers, desert dwellers, and early Christian communities. The only other primary source related to Saint Benedict is a short biography, Dialogue II of *The Dialogues,* attributed to Saint Gregory the Great.

Monastic thinkers, influenced by both the life of Jesus and classical philosophy, recognized that certain sacrifices must be made in order to concentrate on seeking God. They are also necessary for the common good whenever people form a community in which no one can have his own way at all times. Although his rule was written one thousand five hundred years ago, it has endured as a guide for every generation, because human nature has not changed that much. Members of human communities are still trying to find ways to get along with others and be peaceful in their own hearts. Thus, they are still willing to seek and accept some personal discipline in order to become more happy and loving people.

This happiness, not punishment or self-hatred, is the ultimate goal of any discipline, just as when one diets, exercises, or learns a skill. Benedict, in suggesting that life is a continuous Lent, is ever pointing toward the goal that is the end of Lent. To live a Lenten life is to look forward with joyful anticipation toward Easter. As each Lent culminates not with crucifixion but with resurrection, each Lenten life is also lived to transform and transcend one's own death and find eternal joy.

This book uses an adapted version of Father Boniface Verheyen, OSB's translation of *The Rule of Saint Benedict,* copyright 1949, with permission of Saint Benedict's Abbey, Atchison, Kansas.

Texts from the *Dialogues of Saint Gregory* are the author's own versions of the Latin text.

PART I

~~~~~~

READINGS for LENT

DAY 1

The Lenten Life

*T*he life of monastics ought always to be a Lenten observance. However, since such virtue is that of few, we advise that during these days of Lent they guard their lives with all purity and at the same time wash away during these holy days all the shortcomings of other times.

RULE OF SAINT BENEDICT, 49:1–3

SCRIPTURE

For the LORD will again take delight in prospering you, just as he delighted in prospering your ancestors, when you obey the LORD your God by observing his commandments and decrees that are written in this book of the law, because you turn to the LORD your God with all your heart and with all your soul. Surely, this commandment that I am commanding you today is not too hard for you, nor is it too far away....No, the word is very near to you; it is in your mouth and in your heart for you to observe....I call heaven and earth to witness against you today that I have set before you life and death, blessings and curses. Choose life so that you and your descendants may live, loving the LORD your God, obeying him, and holding fast to him.

DEUTERONOMY 30:9B–11, 14, 19–20A

PRAYER

God of all my days, guide me in this Lent, forgive me my past failings and help me to become more pure and holy by this special time of grace. May my efforts in this season lead to true and lasting changes for your greater glory.

LENTEN ACTION

As we approach Lent, we recall how easy it is to fall away from the fervor we feel at the beginning of this holy season. Can you recall what you tried to do last year at this time? Check your progress. Ask for forgiveness, forgive yourself, and commit yourself to a new enthusiasm.

DAY 2

Devotion

*T*his will then be worthily done, if we restrain ourselves from all vices. Let us devote ourselves to tearful prayers, to reading and compunction of heart, and to abstinence.

RULE OF SAINT BENEDICT, 49:4

SCRIPTURE

Yet even now, says the LORD, *return to me with all your heart, with fasting, with weeping, and with mourning; rend your hearts and not your clothing. Return to the* LORD, *your God, for he is gracious and merciful, slow to anger, and abounding in steadfast love, and relents from punishing.*

JOEL 2:12–13

PRAYER

Loving God, when I look honestly at my weaknesses and failings, tearful prayer seems all too right. Take me in my sinfulness and hold me in your steadfast love. I know that you care for me as I am, and I ask your help to become more as you would wish me to be.

LENTEN ACTION

Tears and compunction are not something one eagerly desires. For the ancient monastics, it was not a matter of sadness and self-loathing. "Compunction" referred to being pierced through with an overwhelming sense of both the love and the mercy of God. Think about how much God must love you to still hold you as special despite all your flaws and failings. Spend time today recalling a time when you were not your best self: a time of sadness, doubt or sinfulness. Place it before God and try to feel God's love. If tears come, these are the grace-filled tears of which Benedict speaks.

DAY 3

Something Extra

*D*uring these days, therefore, let us add something to the usual amount of our service, special prayers, abstinence from food and drink, that each one offer to God "with the joy of the Holy Ghost," of their own accord, something above the prescribed measure.

RULE OF SAINT BENEDICT, 49:5–6

SCRIPTURE

We always give thanks to God for all of you and mention you in our prayers, constantly remembering before our God and Father your work of faith and labor of love and steadfastness of hope in our Lord Jesus Christ For we know, brothers and sisters beloved by God, that he has chosen you, because our message of the gospel came to you not in word only, but also in power and in the Holy Spirit and with full conviction; just as you know what kind of persons we proved to be among you for your sake. And you became imitators of us and of the Lord, for in spite of persecution you received the word with joy inspired by the Holy Spirit, so that you became an example to all the believers in Macedonia and in Achaia.

1 THESSALONIANS 1: 2–7

PRAYER

I offer you, O God, my simple acts of service and sacrifice. Send forth your spirit that all I do in this season may be done willingly and happily. Help me always to be grateful and joyful, and to remember those who have nothing beyond the essentials and who sacrifice daily by their suffering.

LENTEN ACTION

Sacrifice is what we most commonly associate with Lent. It is not a mere "giving up" but a self-denial that reminds us of our temptations to fulfill our own wills and pleasures. Think carefully about what you will offer in the way of sacrifice this Lent. Make it something that will keep you mindful of your human desires and, when you are tempted to indulge in it, to use it as a reminder of God's desire for your holiness. Perhaps you may even experience some bit of joy in your sacrifice.

DAY 4

Sharing the Journey

*L*et each one, however, make known to the abbot what is offered and let it be done with his approval and blessing; because what is done without permission of the spiritual leader will be imputed to presumption and vain glory, and not to merit. Therefore, let all be done with the approval of the abbot.

RULE OF SAINT BENEDICT, 49:8–10

SCRIPTURE

If you love to listen you will gain knowledge, and if you pay attention you will become wise. Stand in the company of the elders. Who is wise? Attach yourself to such a one. Be ready to listen to every godly discourse, and let no wise proverbs escape you. If you see an intelligent person, rise early to visit him; let your foot wear out his doorstep. Reflect on the statutes of the LORD, and meditate at all times on his commandments. It is he who will give insight to your mind, and your desire for wisdom will be granted.

SIRACH 6: 33–37

PRAYER

All-seeing God, you know what is in my heart. Grant me the courage to reveal myself humbly to others as well, and to listen willingly to the guidance of those whom I believe to speak for you. Inspire all those who act as spiritual friends to others and keep them attentive to you.

LENTEN ACTION

Benedict makes sure that no one acts as his or her own guide in the spiritual life. The guide prevents one from following in a way that is based solely on one's own perceptions of the self, or trying to take on practices that are excessive or unhelpful. Share your Lenten plans with loved ones and spiritual advisors, get their perspective on what they think might be best for you, and listen humbly to their advice.

DAY 5

The Instruments of Good Works

*I*n the first place to love the Lord God with the whole heart, the whole soul, the whole strength, then, one's neighbor as one's self.

RULE OF SAINT BENEDICT, 4:1–2

SCRIPTURE

The tempter came and said to him, "If you are the Son of God, command these stones to become loaves of bread." But he answered, "It is written, 'One does not live by bread alone, but by every word that comes from the mouth of God.' Then the devil took him to the holy city and placed him on the pinnacle of the temple, saying to him, "If you are the Son of God, throw yourself down; for it is written, 'He will command his angels concerning you,' and 'On their hands they will bear you up, so that you will not dash your foot against a stone.'" Jesus said to him, "Again it is written, 'Do not put the Lord your God to the test.' Again, the devil took him to a very high mountain and showed him all the kingdoms of the world and their splendor; and he said to him, "All these I will give you, if you will fall down and worship me." Jesus said to him, "Away with you, Satan! For it is written, 'Worship the Lord your God, and serve only him.'" Then the devil left him, and suddenly angels came and waited on him.

MATTHEW 4: 3–11

PRAYER

Almighty God, I know that I can never love as you love, but I want to offer myself as wholeheartedly as I am able. Help me to put aside my distractions and focus instead on you and on my neighbors. Deliver me from despair or weakness in the face of my temptations and strengthen me in all I do today.

LENTEN ACTION

Benedict uses one of his first chapters to enumerate a long list of instruments or tools that one must cultivate in order to lead a spiritual life. He begins with the great commandment of love. Every follower of God would insist that he or she loves God, but what does that mean for you? What other loves sometimes get in the way? This Sunday's Gospel reminds us that even Jesus was tempted by the devil to put his own comfort and desires first. At the same time, we cannot love another unless we love ourselves. Jesus could respond to the devil because he was secure in knowing God loved and protected him. Think today about a particular temptation of desire or of attitude that you battle. Is this behavior indicative of an anger or emptiness in yourself?

DAY 6

Keeping the Commandments

*T*hen, not to kill...Not to commit adultery...Not to steal...
Not to covet...Not to bear false witness...To honor all.
And, what one would not have done to one's self, not to do
to another.

RULE OF SAINT BENEDICT, 4:3–9

SCRIPTURE

Moses came and told the people all the words of the LORD and all the ordinances; and all the people answered with one voice, and said, "All the words that the LORD has spoken we will do." And Moses wrote down all the words of the LORD.…Then he took the book of the covenant, and read it in the hearing of the people; and they said, "All that the LORD has spoken we will do, and we will be obedient." Moses took the blood and dashed it on the people, and said, "See the blood of the covenant that the LORD has made with you in accordance with all these words."

EXODUS 24: 3–4A, 7–8

PRAYER

God of Moses, you have given us your commandments to help us live good lives. Forgive my sins against them and renew your covenant in my heart. Thank you for the gift of your Son and the blood he shed to proclaim your faithfulness in spite of the weakness of your people.

LENTEN ACTION

The commandments seem so huge. It is easy to be pleased with the innocence of having never killed anyone or committed adultery or stolen. Stretch your notion of these a little today. Do you envy another's success and say things that aren't exactly lies but cast a disparaging light on a person? Do you find yourself competing in some subtle ways for the attention or affection of another? Do you endanger the life of yourself or others by reckless habits? We may not be breaking commandments in big ways, but we are often bending them to our own benefit. Think about these commandments today and pay attention to any actions that are not really in keeping with them.

DAY 7

Controlling the Body

*T*o deny one's self in order to follow Christ. To chastise the body...Not to seek after pleasures.

RULE OF SAINT BENEDICT, 4:10–13

SCRIPTURE

I do it all for the sake of the gospel, so that I may share in its blessings. Do you not know that in a race the runners all compete, but only one receives the prize? Run in such a way that you may win it. Athletes exercise self-control in all things; they do it to receive a perishable wreath, but we an imperishable one. So I do not run aimlessly, nor do I box as though beating the air; but I punish my body and enslave it, so that after proclaiming to others I myself should not be disqualified.

1 CORINTHIANS 9:23–27

PRAYER

God, you are the prize toward which I run. As I discipline my body and spirit in this Lent, give me strength and an attitude of willingness to accept the pain that results in gain. I offer my self-denial for those whose lives are filled with suffering and who know no pleasures.

LENTEN ACTION

Saint Benedict's rule is not masochistic. There are no extraordinary physical punishments or radical penitential practices. It is, in fact, very moderate and reasonable in its diet, sleep, material resources, relationships, and other matters of personal well-being. It does, however, recognize that a healthy human being does not give in to every desire for pleasure. Consider denying yourself some little pleasures throughout this season. It doesn't have to be the same thing every day. Take note of these things that you would like to do or have but can do without and, as you pass them by, say a prayer for greater awareness of God, and God's suffering children, in that moment.

DAY 8

Works of Mercy

*T*o relieve the poor...To clothe the naked...To visit the sick...To bury the dead...To help in trouble...To console the sorrowing.

RULE OF SAINT BENEDICT, 4:14–19

SCRIPTURE

"Then the king will say to those at his right hand, 'Come, you that are blessed by my Father, inherit the kingdom prepared for you from the foundation of the world; for I was hungry and you gave me food, I was thirsty and you gave me something to drink, I was a stranger and you welcomed me, I was naked and you gave me clothing, I was sick and you took care of me, I was in prison and you visited me.' Then the righteous will answer him, 'Lord, when was it that we saw you hungry and gave you food, or thirsty and gave you something to drink? And when was it that we saw you a stranger and welcomed you, or naked and gave you clothing? And when was it that we saw you sick or in prison and visited you?' And the king will answer them, 'Truly I tell you, just as you did it to one of the least of these who are members of my family, you did it to me.'"

MATTHEW 25:34–41

PRAYER

God of the poor and lowly, you love those in need and want me to love them, too. Keep me aware of your many suffering children and help me to be generous in caring for them. Help me to see your face in each of theirs so that I may be counted among the righteous and enter the kingdom with all those whom I have served.

LENTEN ACTION

The next list provided is that of the "works of mercy." Lent should include both personal improvement and the improvement of the conditions of others. As you are fasting or skipping some personal refreshment or entertainment, pray for those who do not have the luxury of giving up anything. Give the money you would have spent to a charity that serves those in need.

DAY 9

Preferring Christ

o hold one's self aloof from worldly ways...To prefer nothing to the love of Christ.

RULE OF SAINT BENEDICT, 4:20–21

SCRIPTURE

I appeal to you therefore, brothers and sisters, by the mercies of God, to present your bodies as a living sacrifice, holy and acceptable to God, which is your spiritual worship. Do not be conformed to this world, but be transformed by the renewing of your minds, so that you may discern what is the will of God—what is good and acceptable and perfect. For by the grace given to me I say to everyone among you not to think of yourself more highly than you ought to think, but to think with sober judgment, each according to the measure of faith that God has assigned.

ROMANS 12: 1–3

PRAYER

I want to love you, God, above everything else, but sometimes I stray from the path. Forgive me those times when I have preferred myself to you and chosen sinful ways. Fill me with the grace to always make your love the love that I choose above anything.

LENTEN ACTION

A holy person is not one aloof from the world in the sense of being oblivious to its cares and needs. A holy person cares deeply about all of God's creation, but holds it in right perspective, not succumbing to its basest "ways," which promote greed, selfishness or the denigration of others. Take note of the advertising you see today. What does it convey about the world's ways? Do you sometimes prefer choices that are exploitative of others, damaging to the environment, or otherwise opposed to Christ's love for the world? Identify and pray about these.

DAY 10

Do Unto Others

*N*ot to give way to anger. Not to foster a desire for revenge. Not to entertain deceit in the heart. Not to make a false peace. Not to forsake charity.

RULE OF SAINT BENEDICT, 4:22–26

SCRIPTURE

Fools show their anger at once, but the prudent ignore an insult. Whoever speaks the truth gives honest evidence, but a false witness speaks deceitfully. Rash words are like sword thrusts, but the tongue of the wise brings healing. Truthful lips endure forever, but a lying tongue lasts only a moment. Deceit is in the mind of those who plan evil, but those who counsel peace have joy.

PROVERBS 12: 16–20

PRAYER

Forgiving God, you have been so kind and compassionate to me. Help me to show those same feelings toward others. Help me to see those who have hurt me in a new light and to never turn away from those who need my love.

LENTEN ACTION

Human relationships are very important. Benedict points out in his chapter on hospitality that Christ must be seen in everyone. This is especially challenging in dealing with those for whom we do not have a natural affinity. Think of someone with whom you easily become angry or from whom you have become estranged. Pray over that relationship today and ask God's healing for any anger or vengeful feelings in your heart. Pray also for that other person, not with a self-centered prayer that they will see the error of their ways, but pray for them as they are and with a sense of genuine caring.

DAY 11

To Tell the Truth

*N*ot to swear, lest perchance one swear falsely. To speak the truth with heart and tongue.

RULE OF SAINT BENEDICT, 4:27–28

SCRIPTURE

"Again, you have heard that it was said to those of ancient times, 'You shall not swear falsely, but carry out the vows you have made to the Lord.' But I say to you, Do not swear at all, either by heaven, for it is the throne of God, or by the earth, for it is his footstool, or by Jerusalem, for it is the city of the great King. And do not swear by your head, for you cannot make one hair white or black. Let your word be 'Yes, Yes' or 'No, No'; anything more than this comes from the evil one."

MATTHEW 5: 33–37

PRAYER

All-knowing God, I can never lie to you because you know what is in my heart. Help me to make my tongue a more honest reflection of my heart, and my heart a more honest reflection of how you would have me live.

LENTEN ACTION

No one can say that they never lie. Sometimes we want to spare the feelings of another or downplay our own failings or our neglect of responsibility. Neither can anyone claim or promise always to tell the entire truth with no filtering. Perhaps the better question is to ask how honest you are. Do you sometimes go along with the conversation even though you have a different perception of the situation or person being discussed? Pay attention to your conversations today. If you realize you are not telling the truth, stop and rethink your comment, then pray for forgiveness.

DAY 12

Transfigured in Light

*T*wo of the brothers, in different places, saw the same vision.] They both saw a road that was carpeted and glowing with countless lamps. It stretched eastward from the monastery up into heaven. Above them was a man in shining garments who asked them if they knew who had taken this road. When they said they did not, he said, "This is the road taken by blessed Benedict, the Lord's beloved, when he went to heaven." Thus, while the brethren who were with Benedict witnessed his death, those who were absent knew about it through the sign he had promised them.

DIALOGUES II, XXVII

SCRIPTURE

Six days later, Jesus took with him Peter and James and his brother John and led them up a high mountain, by themselves. And he was transfigured before them, and his face shone like the sun, and his clothes became dazzling white. Suddenly there appeared to them Moses and Elijah, talking with him. Then Peter said to Jesus, "Lord, it is good for us to be here; if you wish, I will make three dwellings here, one for you, one for Moses, and one for Elijah." While he was still speaking, suddenly a bright cloud overshadowed them, and from the cloud a voice said, "This is my Son, the Beloved; with him I am well pleased; listen to him!" When the disciples heard this, they fell to the ground and were overcome by fear. But Jesus came and touched them, saying, "Get up and do not be afraid." And when they looked up, they saw no one except Jesus himself alone.

MATTHEW 17: 1–8

PRAYER

Glorious God, in the midst of our Lent, you show us your great power and love. Help me to see your glory and not merely bask in the light, but return to the everyday world to proclaim you. Calm my fears so that I, too, may be one in whom you are well pleased.

LENTEN ACTION

The Sunday gospels follow the temptation with the transfiguration. As Jesus overcame the things that might take him from his task, he was strengthened by the presence of the lawgiver and prophet, perhaps encouraging him to bring God's people to the next level. Perhaps they told him not to be afraid, thus giving him the courage to say the same to his disciples and to tell them they must return to harsh reality. Pay attention to light today, as when you turn on a light or open a shade. See the world being transfigured as you look at sun and shadow. As you look at other people, both familiar and strangers, imagine them glorified by divine light and God expressing pleasure in their existence.

DAY 13

Love One Another

*N*ot to return evil for evil...To do no injury, even patiently to bear the injury done us. To love one's enemies. Not to curse them that curse us, but rather to bless them. To bear persecution for justice sake.

RULE OF SAINT BENEDICT, 4:29–33

SCRIPTURE

Do not repay evil for evil or abuse for abuse; but, on the contrary, repay with a blessing. It is for this that you were called — that you might inherit a blessing. For "Those who desire life and desire to see good days, let them keep their tongues from evil and their lips from speaking deceit; let them turn away from evil and do good; let them seek peace and pursue it. For the eyes of the Lord are on the righteous, and his ears are open to their prayer. But the face of the Lord is against those who do evil." Now who will harm you if you are eager to do what is good? But even if you do suffer for doing what is right, you are blessed. Do not fear what they fear, and do not be intimidated, but in your hearts sanctify Christ as Lord. Always be ready to make your defense to anyone who demands from you an accounting for the hope that is in you; yet do it with gentleness and reverence. Keep your conscience clear, so that, when you are maligned, those who abuse you for your good conduct in Christ may be put to shame.

1 PETER: 3:9–16

PRAYER

Merciful God, even in the ultimate persecution of crucifixion, your Son not only endured but forgave. Place in my heart the strength to accept injury and the grace to forgive. Bless all those who are tortured by others, and those who torture themselves with feelings of hatred for those who have hurt them.

LENTEN ACTION

Ours is a world where there seems to be great energy around divisions of ethnicity, political views, religion, and anything else where we can draw the lines of a clear "us versus them." Make a list, not just of those you would consider actual enemies, but of people or groups with whom you very strongly disagree, those who have wronged you, those you think want to harm you. Look at the list, stopping at each one to say a short prayer of blessing.

DAY 14

TUESDAY OF THE SECOND WEEK OF LENT

Temperate Living

*N*ot to be proud. Not to be given to wine. Not to be a great eater. Not to be drowsy. Not to be slothful. Not to be a murmurer. Not to be a detractor.

RULE OF SAINT BENEDICT, 4:34–38

SCRIPTURE

But as for you, teach what is consistent with sound doctrine. Tell the older men to be temperate, serious, prudent, and sound in faith, in love, and in endurance. Likewise, tell the older women to be reverent in behavior, not to be slanderers or slaves to drink; they are to teach what is good, so that they may encourage the young women to love their husbands, to love their children, to be self-controlled, chaste, good managers of the household, kind, being submissive to their husbands, so that the word of God may not be discredited. Likewise, urge the younger men to be self-controlled. Show yourself in all respects a model of good works, and in your teaching show integrity, gravity, and sound speech that cannot be censured; then any opponent will be put to shame, having nothing evil to say of us.

TITUS 2: 1–8

PRAYER

Creator God, you have made us in your image, but our human bodies are weak and frail. I know that I often give in to my baser instincts, and I ask your forgiveness for those times when I have not tempered my body and emotions with wisdom. Bless those who are addicted physically or emotionally and bring them to wholeness.

LENTEN ACTION

This section of the list deals with a variety of personal flaws. They were among the failings addressed by early philosophers and desert dwellers as things that draw one away from the common good and distract from contemplation of the divine. Go prayerfully over this group and pick the one you find most challenging in your own life. Pay special attention to it today and try not only to avoid it but also to do something positive to counteract it.

DAY 15

We Die to Live Forever

To put one's trust in God. To refer what good they see in themselves, not to self, but to God. But as to any evil in themselves, let them be convinced that it is their own and charge it to themselves. To fear the day of judgment. To be in dread of hell. To desire eternal life with all spiritual longing. To keep death before one's eyes daily.

RULE OF SAINT BENEDICT, 4:41–47

SCRIPTURE

But God, who is rich in mercy, out of the great love with which he loved us even when we were dead through our trespasses, made us alive together with Christ—by grace you have been saved—and raised us up with him and seated us with him in the heavenly places in Christ Jesus, so that in the ages to come he might show the immeasurable riches of his grace in kindness toward us in Christ Jesus. For by grace you have been saved through faith, and this is not your own doing; it is the gift of God—not the result of works, so that no one may boast. For we are what he has made us, created in Christ Jesus for good works, which God prepared beforehand to be our way of life.

EPHESIANS 2: 4–10

PRAYER

Eternal God, my life is but a brief moment and everything in it comes from you and returns to you. I praise and thank you for your uncountable gifts to me, and I pray that I may use them for your praise until I stand before you at death. I do desire eternal life and ask your blessing now and at the hour of my death.

LENTEN ACTION

To keep death daily before one's eyes is not a command to a morbid preoccupation with dying. Rather it is meant to encourage the reader to be mindful of what really matters, where we come from and where we are going. It is a reminder that every act of every day is leading to the moment of judgment, when we will be accountable for what we have done with our lives. Imagine your own death and what others might be thinking and feeling. How do you think you will be remembered? Is this the way you want to be remembered? Does anything need to change now?

DAY 16

God's Eye Is on Us

To keep a constant watch over the actions of our life. To hold as certain that God sees us everywhere. To dash at once against Christ the evil thoughts which rise in one's heart. And to disclose them to our spiritual guide.

RULE OF SAINT BENEDICT, 4:48–50

SCRIPTURE

The eyes of the LORD are in every place, keeping watch on the evil and the good. A gentle tongue is a tree of life, but perverseness in it breaks the spirit. A fool despises a parent's instruction, but the one who heeds admonition is prudent.

PROVERBS 15:3–5

PRAYER

All-knowing God, I am always in your loving sight. Keep me mindful of this truth so that I will act only in accordance with your will. May all who see me this day see you in me.

LENTEN ACTION

If we believe that God is always with us, we must be mindful of all our private actions and thoughts. Pay particular attention today to where your thoughts go in the unguarded moments of the day. Are they thoughts that would be pleasing to God, or even to yourself if you really stopped and thought about them? Are there certain types of thoughts that seem to dominate your thinking? Try to identify one recurring theme that you do not find edifying and take steps to divert it by turning it to a moment of prayer instead.

DAY 17

Silence Is Golden

*T*o guard one's tongue against bad and wicked speech. Not to love much speaking. Not to speak useless words and such as provoke laughter. Not to love much or boisterous laughter.

RULE OF SAINT BENEDICT, 4:51–54

SCRIPTURE

Do not winnow in every wind, or follow every path. Stand firm for what you know, and let your speech be consistent. Be quick to hear, but deliberate in answering. If you know what to say, answer your neighbor; but if not, put your hand over your mouth. Honor and dishonor come from speaking, and the tongue of mortals may be their downfall.

SIRACH 5: 9–13

PRAYER

God, you gave me lips to proclaim your praise and to teach and comfort others. Forgive me for the times when I have used my speech in ways that do not give praise. Guard my words today, make them humble and helpful. May I lead others to you and bring them joy and peace.

LENTEN ACTION

This part of the list does not suggest that the holy person is silent and morose. It simply points out that most of us speak more often than we need to speak, and say things that might better be left unsaid. Listen carefully to yourself today. Think before you speak. Speak gently and truthfully.

DAY 18

Pray Always

To listen willingly to holy reading. To apply one's self often to prayer.

RULE OF SAINT BENEDICT, 4:55–56

SCRIPTURE

In the days of his flesh, Jesus offered up prayers and supplications, with loud cries and tears, to the one who was able to save him from death, and he was heard because of his reverent submission. Although he was a Son, he learned obedience through what he suffered; and having been made perfect, he became the source of eternal salvation for all who obey him.

HEBREWS 5: 7–9

PRAYER

Eternal Word and Spirit, incline my ear to your revelation in Scripture and to your personal words to me in prayer. Make me attentive to your message and eager to take the time to hear it.

LENTEN ACTION

The discipline of daily prayer is essential in keeping one focused on God. Read a short reading from Scripture each day. Stop for personal prayer each morning and evening, and at other brief intervals throughout the day if possible.

DAY 19

I Confess

*T*o confess one's past sins to God daily in prayer with sighs and tears, and to amend them for the future.

RULE OF SAINT BENEDICT, 4:57–58

SCRIPTURE

Jesus said to her, "Everyone who drinks of this water will be thirsty again, but those who drink of the water that I will give them will never be thirsty. The water that I will give will become in them a spring of water gushing up to eternal life." The woman said to him, "Sir, give me this water, so that I may never be thirsty or have to keep coming here to draw water."

Jesus said to her, "Go, call your husband, and come back." The woman answered him, "I have no husband." Jesus said to her, "You are right in saying, 'I have no husband'; for you have had five husbands, and the one you have now is not your husband. What you have said is true!" The woman said to him, "Sir, I see that you are a prophet."…"I know that Messiah is coming" (who is called Christ). "When he comes, he will proclaim all things to us." Jesus said to her, "I am he, the one who is speaking to you."

JOHN 4:13–19, 25–26

PRAYER

Forgiving God, you already know all my sins and failings, but I must face them and acknowledge them. I am truly sorry for all that I have done that was not as you would have wanted me to do. Sprinkle me with the healing waters of your mercy as I promise to go forward in holiness and abandon sinful ways. Bless in a special way all those whom I have hurt by my actions.

LENTEN ACTION

God certainly does not need to receive any information from us in order to know what we have done or failed to do. Confessing our failings is for the purpose of bringing them to our own consciousness, acknowledging why they were failings, and strengthening our resolve to avoid them in the future. Is there someone besides God to whom you need to apologize today? Is there something you can do to right a past wrong?

DAY 20

Thy Will Be Done

ot to fulfill the desires of the flesh. To hate one's own will. To obey the commands of the abbot in all things, even though he himself (which Heaven forbid) act otherwise, mindful of that precept of the Lord: "What they say, do ye; what they do, do ye not." Not to desire to be called holy before one is; but to be holy first, that one may be truly so called.

RULE OF SAINT BENEDICT, 4:59–62

SCRIPTURE

For you were called to freedom, brothers and sisters; only do not use your freedom as an opportunity for self-indulgence, but through love become slaves to one another. For the whole law is summed up in a single commandment, "You shall love your neighbor as yourself." If, however, you bite and devour one another, take care that you are not consumed by one another. Live by the Spirit, I say, and do not gratify the desires of the flesh. For what the flesh desires is opposed to the Spirit, and what the Spirit desires is opposed to the flesh; for these are opposed to each other, to prevent you from doing what you want.

GALATIANS 5: 13–17

PRAYER

All-holy God, you gave us the perfect example to be followed in the life and death of your Son, Jesus. Grant that I may always look only to him and to seek holiness with all my being. Grant that I may be an example of holy living in everything that I do and say today.

LENTEN ACTION

This segment of the list has more to do with not being one's own master than it has to do with never wanting anything good for yourself. The common good of one's family, religious community, or any other set of human relationships should dictate our actions more than what we might call "self will." At this midpoint of Lent, check in with your significant others to see how they think you are doing in your efforts at transformation.

DAY 21

Curbing the Passions

*T*o fulfill daily the commandments of God by works. To love chastity. To hate no one. Not to be jealous; not to entertain envy. Not to love strife. Not to love pride.

RULE OF SAINT BENEDICT, 4:63–69

SCRIPTURE

Who is wise and understanding among you? Show by your good life that your works are done with gentleness born of wisdom. But if you have bitter envy and selfish ambition in your hearts, do not be boastful and false to the truth. Such wisdom does not come down from above, but is earthly, unspiritual, devilish.

For where there is envy and selfish ambition, there will also be disorder and wickedness of every kind. But the wisdom from above is first pure, then peaceable, gentle, willing to yield, full of mercy and good fruits, without a trace of partiality or hypocrisy. And a harvest of righteousness is sown in peace for those who make peace.

JAMES 3: 13–18

PRAYER

God who can see into my heart, you know that there are feelings there which can lead to sin and discord. Forgive me my sinful thoughts and lead me toward charity and the love of your commands. Bless those who are enslaved by their feelings of pride or envy or hatred and bring them into the light of your love.

LENTEN ACTION

Earlier in his listing, Benedict addresses some of the so-called "deadly sins" which have to do with behaviors such as gluttony and grumbling. The effects of these are often outwardly evident. There are other sins, however, which are not so apparent. Toward the end of the list, Benedict asks his followers to address those that may hide in the soul. It is no accident that they follow the line about being called holy before one truly is holy. Only the mature Christian can address the internal conditions honestly. Examine this list as well, and find the one that is most challenging. Again pay attention to how it manifests in your daily life and make efforts to combat it.

DAY 22

Crossing the Generation Gap

To honor the aged.
To love the younger.

RULE OF SAINT BENEDICT, 4:70–71

SCRIPTURE

Then little children were being brought to him in order that he might lay his hands on them and pray. The disciples spoke sternly to those who brought them; but Jesus said, "Let the little children come to me, and do not stop them; for it is to such as these that the kingdom of heaven belongs." And he laid his hands on them and went on his way.

MATTHEW 19:13–15

PRAYER

God of all people, you ask us to share your special concern for those who are weak and in need of protection and care. Bless the elders and the children with loving providers and the respect and nurturing that will reflect your love for them. Make me patient and caring in all my encounters with them.

LENTEN ACTION

This may seem a bit anti-climactic after the magnitude of some of the other challenges on the list. Benedict lived in a community that tried to harmonize the needs and spirits of people of all ages. This is not just about being charitable to the more vulnerable, but about accepting the wisdom and contribution of all. Older people can be very critical of the direction they think the world is going and young people can be very impatient with those they feel are impeding them with outdated ideas and expectations. Give to a charity that cares for the young or old in need of assistance, but also think about your own attitudes and how you convey your feelings about people of other generations.

DAY 23

Reconciliation

*T*o pray for one's enemies in the love of Christ. To make peace with an adversary before the setting of the sun.

RULE OF SAINT BENEDICT, 4:72–73

SCRIPTURE

So then, putting away falsehood, let all of us speak the truth to our neighbors, for we are members of one another. Be angry but do not sin; do not let the sun go down on your anger, and do not make room for the devil. Thieves must give up stealing; rather let them labor and work honestly with their own hands, so as to have something to share with the needy.

Let no evil talk come out of your mouths, but only what is useful for building up, as there is need, so that your words may give grace to those who hear. And do not grieve the Holy Spirit of God, with which you were marked with a seal for the day of redemption. Put away from you all bitterness and wrath and anger and wrangling and slander, together with all malice, and be kind to one another, tenderhearted, forgiving one another, as God in Christ has forgiven you.

EPHESIANS 4: 25–32

PRAYER

God of peace, you would have us love each other as you love each of us. Bless those whom I have found hard to love, help me to be a person of peace and reconciliation, and enlighten all people with love so that our fractured and violent world may be blessed with peace.

LENTEN ACTION

Benedict returns once again to the discord with which he has shown such concern. To love those we found unlovable is the manifestation of having removed much of the sinfulness in ourselves. Thus, we will be able to see them in a new light and love them as Christ has loved us. At the end of the day, pray for anyone with whom you have had a dispute. If possible, try to make peace with them. It is a good practice in a household to ask one another's forgiveness at the end of each day. There may also be those with whom you can no longer reconcile in the flesh. God's day has no sundown; you can still be reconciled in your heart.

DAY 24

The Craft of Living

*B*ehold, these are the instruments of the spiritual art, which, if they have been applied without ceasing day and night and approved on judgment day, will merit for us from the Lord that reward which He has promised: "The eye has not seen, nor the ear heard, neither has it entered into the heart of humans, what things God has prepared for them that love Him."

RULE OF SAINT BENEDICT, 4:75–77

SCRIPTURE

But we speak God's wisdom, secret and hidden, which God decreed before the ages for our glory. None of the rulers of this

age understood this; for if they had, they would not have cruci-
fied the Lord of glory. But, as it is written, "What no eye has
seen, nor ear heard, nor the human heart conceived, what God
has prepared for those who love him"—these things God has
revealed to us through the Spirit; for the Spirit searches every-
thing, even the depths of God. For what human being knows
what is truly human except the human spirit that is within? So
also no one comprehends what is truly God's except the Spirit
of God. Now we have received not the spirit of the world, but
the Spirit that is from God, so that we may understand the
gifts bestowed on us by God.

1 CORINTHIANS 2: 7–12

PRAYER

God of heaven and earth, I look forward with all my heart to
the unimaginable glory of your kingdom. As I look forward
through Lent to Easter, I commit myself anew to using my
life to proclaim your kingdom and look forward to my own
death and resurrection. Give me your grace and lead me to
the glory you have promised.

LENTEN ACTION

All of the things Saint Benedict identifies in Chapter 4 are
tools for practicing the most important of crafts. Tools help
us to do a job well and with greater ease and precision. Everyone has a different degree of skill and talent for different
tools. Go prayerfully over the entire list today. Pick the one
with which you feel most skilled and thank God for it. Try
to use it consciously today. Pick the one that you find most
unwieldy and ask God's aid in increasing your ability.

DAY 25

Keeping a Helpful Workshop

ut the workshop in which we perform all these works with diligence is the enclosure of the monastery, and stability in the community.

RULE OF SAINT BENEDICT, 4:78

SCRIPTURE

All who believed were together and had all things in common; they would sell their possessions and goods and distribute the proceeds to all, as any had need. Day by day, as they spent much time together in the temple, they broke bread at home and ate their food with glad and generous hearts, praising God and having the goodwill of all the people.

ACTS 2:44–47

PRAYER

Generous God, you have given me not only tools for doing your will, but a workshop of other people who share their gifts with me as well. Bless my household, my faith community, my family, friends, and co-workers, and all with whom I share some lasting relationship. Keep them faithful to your will so that together we may build your kingdom.

LENTEN ACTION

Everyone has both unique tools and a unique environment in which to use them. It is necessary to have the support of others to be our most Christ-like selves. What is your workshop like? Go over the list again as yesterday, but this time think about your own household or most important personal relationships. In which tools are you, as a group, most strong? What are the weakest tools among this group of persons, or what tools are not being used well? What should you do about them?

DAY 26

Returning to God

*A*nd never to despair of God's mercy.

RULE OF SAINT BENEDICT, 4:74

SCRIPTURE

But while he was still far off, his father saw him and was filled with compassion; he ran and put his arms around him and kissed him....But [the elder son] answered his father, "Listen! For all these years I have been working like a slave for you, and I have never disobeyed your command; yet you have never given me even a young goat so that I might celebrate with my friends. But when this son of yours came back, who has devoured your property with prostitutes, you killed the fatted calf for him!"

Then the father said to him, "Son, you are always with me, and all that is mine is yours. But we had to celebrate and rejoice, because this brother of yours was dead and has come to life; he was lost and has been found."

LUKE 15:20B, 29–32

PRAYER

Merciful and loving God, I know that, no matter how many times I fall, you are always waiting to lift me up and hold me. When I feel most unlovable, show me your love. When I feel I cannot face you, help me see your compassionate face looking kindly at me. Keep me from all fear and despair as I make my way slowly and awkwardly toward you this Lent.

LENTEN ACTION

This last item on the list is the most important. After reading about so many things at which we are so imperfect, Benedict wants to uplift the reader. He does not expect anyone to master all these instructions in one lifetime, so he reminds those who are striving toward perfection that they will never achieve it. The list is not a checklist that requires a perfect score for salvation. If you feel you aren't as good as you would like to be at any of the others, then you should at least master this one. The believer is commanded, alongside all these other commandments, not to despair. The mercy of God is the culmination of the list. Think of a time when you despaired, or were on the verge of despair. How did you feel the presence and love of God? What kept you going? Pray in thanksgiving for that gift of salvation and keep it in mind whenever you are tempted to give up or give in.

DAY 27

The Way of Humility

*T*he first degree of humility, then, is that one always have the fear of God before his/her eyes, shunning all forgetfulness, and be ever mindful of all that God has commanded, that one always consider in the mind how those who despise God will burn in hell for their sins, and that life everlasting is prepared for those who fear God.

RULE OF SAINT BENEDICT, 7:10–11

SCRIPTURE

The works of his hands are faithful and just; all his precepts are trustworthy. They are established forever and ever, to be performed with faithfulness and uprightness. He sent redemption to his people; he has commanded his covenant forever. Holy and awesome is his name. The fear of the LORD is the beginning of wisdom; all those who practice it have a good understanding. His praise endures forever.

PSALM 111:7–10

PRAYER

Almighty God, I do not fear you as one who would punish or reject, but I stand in awe of your power and your dominion over all that exists. Be with me in my quest for humility as you were with your Son, Jesus, in his last days of total abandonment of self. I offer you all that I am and do in humbleness of heart.

LENTEN ACTION

For those who would truly follow the way of Jesus, Saint Benedict offers another "list" for right living in his chapter on humility. Humility is the virtue he identifies as essential for living a life that is in harmony with God's plan and will bring about the fullness of God's kingdom. The first realization one must have is that God is God and we are not. Ultimately, we are not the masters of our lives and must be constantly aware that all is from God and for God. What do you think of when you think of "humility?" How is it different from "fear of the Lord?" Try to bring these concepts together in your mind and think about whether you desire true humility. Pray for this gift today.

DAY 28

Be It Done According to Your Word

The second degree of humility is, when they love not their own will, nor are pleased to fulfill their own desires but by deeds carry out that word of the Lord which says: "I came not to do My own will but the will of Him that sent Me." It is likewise said: "Self-will has its punishment, but necessity wins the crown."

RULE OF SAINT BENEDICT, 7:31–33

SCRIPTURE

"Everything that the Father gives me will come to me, and anyone who comes to me I will never drive away; for I have come down from heaven, not to do my own will, but the will of him who sent me. And this is the will of him who sent me, that I should lose nothing of all that he has given me, but raise it up on the last day. This is indeed the will of my Father, that all who see the Son and believe in him may have eternal life; and I will raise them up on the last day."

JOHN 6: 37–40

PRAYER

All-powerful God, help me to pray, as your Son, Jesus, and his mother Mary did, that everything be done according to your will. Help me to find something good in all that happens, even if it is not what I wanted to happen. I offer my sufferings and disappointments this day for all who are suffering more intensely and are more in want than I am.

LENTEN ACTION

Once we acknowledge that we do not have total control of our lives, it leads to a realization that we cannot always have things our way. This does not mean we should never want anything or never receive anything, merely that we not focus on the love of our own will. Think about a time when you were disappointed or did not get your way but some good resulted or some lesson was learned. Pray for openness to accept life as it comes, whether it is your will or not.

DAY 29

Christit Became Obedient

The third degree of humility is, that for the love of God
they subject themselves to a superior in all obedience,
imitating the Lord, of whom the Apostle says: "He became
obedient unto death."

RULE OF SAINT BENEDICT, 7:34

SCRIPTURE

Let the same mind be in you that was in Christ Jesus, who, though he was in the form of God, did not regard equality with God as something to be exploited, but emptied himself, taking the form of a slave, being born in human likeness. And being found in human form, he humbled himself and became obedient to the point of death—even death on a cross. Therefore God also highly exalted him and gave him the name that is above every name, so that at the name of Jesus every knee should bend, in heaven and on earth and under the earth, and every tongue should confess that Jesus Christ is Lord, to the glory of God the Father.

PHILIPPIANS 2:5–11

PRAYER

Guide of my life, you have placed others in authority over me as well. Help me to find wise persons and listen humbly to their advice. Bless all who hold authority over others and help them to conform their rule to yours as well.

LENTEN ACTION

Not only do we not always get our own way, there are people who are in positions where their will trumps ours. In an ideal world, they would hold authority because they are wiser or more capable or more spiritual. Saint Benedict wants the seeker of humility to seek these people of "superior" gifts and listen to them. Authority should not be about one person forcing his will on another, but people discerning the will of God and the common good together. Who do you trust with your life? How does that person treat you, and how does that mirror God's care?

DAY 30

Life Is Not Fair

*T*he fourth degree of humility is, that, if hard and distasteful things are commanded, nay, even though injuries are inflicted, they accept them with patience and even temper, and not grow weary or give up, but hold out... And fulfilling the command of the Lord by patience also in adversities and injuries, when struck on the one cheek they turn also the other; the despoiler of their coat they give their cloak also; and when forced to go one mile they go two; with the Apostle Paul they bear with false brethren and "bless those who curse them."

RULE OF SAINT BENEDICT, 7:35–36A, 42–43

SCRIPTURE

"You have heard that it was said, 'An eye for an eye and a tooth for a tooth.' But I say to you, Do not resist an evildoer. But if anyone strikes you on the right cheek, turn the other also; and if anyone wants to sue you and take your coat, give your cloak as well; and if anyone forces you to go one mile, go also the second mile. Give to everyone who begs from you, and do not refuse anyone who wants to borrow from you. You have heard that it was said, 'You shall love your neighbor and hate your enemy.' But I say to you, Love your enemies and pray for those who persecute you, so that you may be children of your Father in heaven."

MATTHEW 5:38–45A

PRAYER

God of love, it is so hard for me to love as you do when I am suffering, especially if I am unjustly mistreated. Help me to remain mindful of your Son's passion and death, and of all who are mistreated and persecuted today. Help me to be gentle and forgiving and to bear all the circumstances of my life with a peaceful heart.

LENTEN ACTION

Humility is not the same as humiliation, but they do overlap. The fourth reality of the journey to humility is that life is not always fair or pleasant. Bad things will happen; people will treat you badly, either accidentally or with malice. There is often little that can be done to control the event or other people. We can control only our response and our trust in God. Think about something that is hard or painful in your life. Is there anything you can actively do to relieve it? Is there anything you can do to change your attitude if you can't change the circumstances? Pray for courage and trust in God.

DAY 31

Baring the Soul

*T*he fifth degree of humility is, when one hides from his abbot none of the evil thoughts, which rise in the heart or the evils committed in secret, but humbly confesses them. Concerning this the Scripture exhorts us, saying: "Reveal your way to the Lord and trust in Him."

RULE OF SAINT BENEDICT, 7:44–45

SCRIPTURE

Great are your judgments and hard to describe; therefore uninstructed souls have gone astray. For when lawless people supposed that they held the holy nation in their power, they themselves lay as captives of darkness and prisoners of long night, shut in under their roofs, exiles from eternal providence. For thinking that in their secret sins they were unobserved behind a dark curtain of forgetfulness, they were scattered, terribly alarmed, and appalled by specters.

WISDOM 17: 1–3

PRAYER

God who knows my very heart, help me to overcome my pride and shame in order to reveal my heart to those who can help me. Walk with me on the way to accepting and healing my most hidden hurts. Give comfort to those who have no one to comfort them and those who are paralyzed by guilt.

LENTEN ACTION

Humility requires us to know ourselves truly, even the most unpleasant parts. It is one thing to acknowledge them inwardly, but another to admit them out loud. This is the height of vulnerability, and yet it is where true acceptance of the self and trust in another occurs. Speak truthfully about yourself to another. Seek counseling or spiritual direction. If your faith tradition has some ritual of confession or reconciliation, be sure to take advantage of this opportunity during Lent.

DAY 32

Acceptance

The sixth degree of humility is when they are content with the meanest and worst of everything, and in all that is enjoined they hold themselves as bad and worthless workers, saying with the Prophet: "I am brought to nothing and I knew it not; I am become as a beast before you, yet I am always with you."

RULE OF SAINT BENEDICT, 7:49–50

SCRIPTURE

When my soul was embittered, when I was pricked in heart, I was stupid and ignorant; I was like a brute beast toward you. Nevertheless I am continually with you; you hold my right hand. You guide me with your counsel, and afterward you will receive me with honor. Whom have I in heaven but you? And there is nothing on earth that I desire other than you. My flesh and my heart may fail, but God is the strength of my heart and my portion forever.

PSALM 73:21–26

PRAYER

Provider God, you have given me so much and I have often failed to use it well. You have asked so little of me, yet I often demand so much of you. I come before you as one who wants with all my heart to be a better steward. Help me to be content with little, to demand nothing as my due and to remember that your love and mercy are all that I need.

LENTEN ACTION

The middle steps of humility are difficult for modern sensibilities because they seem to suggest a total lack of self-esteem and even self-loathing. They are placed here because the person who has faced the truths of the earlier steps and comes face to face with his or her own inadequacies and infidelities will naturally experience a sense of disillusionment and even disgust. How do you feel when you have to settle for something inadequate or when you are not able to do something well? Try to imagine God accepting you as a loving parent accepts a very imperfect gift or artwork held out by a small child.

DAY 33
FIFTH SUNDAY OF LENT

Lowliness

*T*he seventh degree of humility is, when, not only with the tongue they declare, but also in the inmost soul believe, that they are the lowest and vilest of people, humbling themselves and saying with the Prophet: "But I am a worm and no man, the reproach of men and the outcast of the people"...And also: "It is good for me that you have humbled me, that I may learn your commandments."

RULE OF SAINT BENEDICT, 7:51–54

SCRIPTURE

My God, my God, why have you forsaken me? Why are you so far from helping me, from the words of my groaning? O my God, I cry by day, but you do not answer; and by night, but find no rest. Yet you are holy, enthroned on the praises of Israel. In you our ancestors trusted; they trusted, and you delivered them. To you they cried, and were saved; in you they trusted, and were not put to shame. But I am a worm, and not human; scorned by others, and despised by the people. All who see me mock at me; they make mouths at me, they shake their heads; "Commit your cause to the LORD; let him deliver—let him rescue the one in whom he delights!" Yet it was you who took me from the womb; you kept me safe on my mother's breast. On you I was cast from my birth, and since my mother bore me you have been my God.

PSALM 22:1–10

PRAYER

God of power and might, I know that I am but one tiny bit of your creation. Help me to remember that you still hold me as precious. Bless the lowly of our world, the helpless, the persecuted, the abandoned. Help me to see myself in true perspective, to recognize both my insignificance and your merciful love. May I offer my gifts generously, simple as they are, and rejoice in serving others.

LENTEN ACTION

It seems that we often do not turn toward God until we have exhausted all our own resources. Most of the time, we would hardly want to identify ourselves with a worm. Yet this is the psalm that Jesus prayed from the cross. It begins with a cry of desperation, but ends with a reminder that God never abandons even a worm. Who are considered the lowest types of people in our society? Try to think about them with love today and do something to improve their condition, if only a shift in your own attitude toward them.

DAY 34

MONDAY OF THE FIFTH WEEK OF LENT

Grounded in Community

*T*he eighth degree of humility is, when they do nothing but what is sanctioned by the common rule of the monastery and the example of the elders.

RULE OF SAINT BENEDICT, 7:55

SCRIPTURE

Here is my servant, whom I uphold, my chosen, in whom my soul delights; I have put my spirit upon him; he will bring forth justice to the nations. He will not cry or lift up his voice, or make it heard in the street; a bruised reed he will not break, and a dimly burning wick he will not quench; he will faithfully bring forth justice. He will not grow faint or be crushed until he has established justice in the earth; and the coastlands wait for his teaching. Thus says God, the LORD, who created the heavens and stretched them out, who spread out the earth and what comes from it, who gives breath to the people upon it and spirit to those who walk in it: I am the LORD, I have called you in righteousness, I have taken you by the hand and kept you; I have given you as a covenant to the people, a light to the nations.

ISAIAH 42:1–6

PRAYER

God, guiding light of the world, you have graced us with many ways in which we can learn your wisdom. Help me to eagerly embrace your instructions as I have received them through my religion, other cultural institutions and personal relationships. Help me to see the wisdom in them and appreciate the wisdom of those who teach me. Bless all who hold authority that they may be an example of holiness to others.

LENTEN ACTION

Every person is part of a culture that tells them what is expected of responsible members. There may be a need for some changes and adaptations, but the solid values that make a society work will remain. What example have you gotten from the elders? Who have been your most valued guides and what did they teach you?

DAY 35

Keeping It to Yourself

*T*he ninth degree of humility is, when they withhold their tongues from speaking, and keeping silence do not speak until they are asked; for the Scripture shows that "in a multitude of words there shall not want sin."

RULE OF SAINT BENEDICT, 7:56–57

SCRIPTURE

Set a guard over my mouth, O LORD; keep watch over the door of my lips. Do not turn my heart to any evil, to busy myself with wicked deeds in company with those who work iniquity; do not let me eat of their delicacies.

PSALM 141:3–4

PRAYER

God who speaks in silence, your Son was silent before his accusers. Help me to be sparing of speech in order to hear your voice. Forgive me for the times I have sinned by my words and bless all those, especially innocent children, who suffer verbal abuse from others.

LENTEN ACTION

Our world is very short on silence. In times and places where there is little natural noise, we add recorded music or some other form of distraction. Try to turn off some of the noise today. Use the silence to listen to your own thoughts and prayers and especially to be still and listen for the sound of God's voice.

DAY 36

Not That Funny

The tenth degree of humility is when they are not easily moved and quick for laughter, for it is written: "The fool exalts his voice in laughter."

RULE OF SAINT BENEDICT, 7:59

SCRIPTURE

A fool's chatter is like a burden on a journey, but delight is found in the speech of the intelligent. The utterance of a sensible person is sought in the assembly, and they ponder his words in their minds. Like a house in ruins is wisdom to a fool, and to the ignorant, knowledge is talk that has no meaning. To a senseless person education is fetters on his feet, and like manacles on his right hand. A fool raises his voice when he laughs, but the wise smile quietly.

SIRACH 21:16–20

PRAYER

God of all joy, you have given us the wonderful gifts of laughter and happiness. Yet I know that sometimes I laugh when I should not. Bless all those who are teased or insulted, and help me to be more compassionate so that I will not find amusement in the injury or errors of any of your children. Make my laughter gentle and kind.

LENTEN ACTION

This step of humility does not suggest that the holy person has no sense of humor. It does suggest that there are not as many things that should move one to laughter as we might think. We have all known someone who laughed too loud and too much, and we usually do not admire that characteristic and consider it a sign of some deep insecurity. Much of what passes for humor is based on another person being injured, insulted, deceived, or denigrated. Pay attention to humor today in jokes, ads, TV programs, and conversation. What do you laugh at and why? How funny is it really?

DAY 37

Speak Softly

The eleventh degree of humility is, that, when they speak, they speak gently and without laughter, humbly and with gravity, with few and sensible words, and that they be not loud of voice, as it is written: "The wise one is known by the fewness of words."

RULE OF SAINT BENEDICT, 7:60–61

SCRIPTURE

As soon as it was morning, the chief priests held a consultation with the elders and scribes and the whole council. They bound Jesus, led him away, and handed him over to Pilate. Pilate asked him, "Are you the King of the Jews?" He answered him, "You say so." Then the chief priests accused him of many things. Pilate asked him again, "Have you no answer? See how many charges they bring against you." But Jesus made no further reply, so that Pilate was amazed.

MARK 15:1–5

PRAYER

God of wisdom, I long to follow in the way of humility and truth. Calm my heart so that it may be reflected in my speech. Free me from words that hurt or judge others. Let me listen more than I speak and, when I speak to say only what would be pleasing to you and uplifting to others.

LENTEN ACTION

It seems odd that this would be such a high level of humility, but our words are the way in which we most directly convey what is in our hearts. Recall a person you have known whom you considered holy. Was that person noisy? Did he or she speak a lot of empty words? When he or she was happy, how was this happiness expressed? Perhaps this quietude that Benedict is proposing is really a much better indicator of holiness than we might first suspect. Think of that holy mentor frequently today. Try to imitate him or her in your own actions.

DAY 38

Walking the Walk

*T*he twelfth degree of humility is when they are not only humble of heart, but always let it appear also in their whole exterior to all that see them; namely, at the Work of God, in the garden, on a journey, in the field, or wherever they may be, sitting, walking, or standing, let them always have the head bowed down, eyes fixed on the ground.

RULE OF SAINT BENEDICT, 7:62–63

SCRIPTURE

For he grew up before him like a young plant, and like a root out of dry ground; he had no form or majesty that we should look at him, nothing in his appearance that we should desire him. He was despised and rejected by others; a man of suffering and acquainted with infirmity; and as one from whom others hide their faces he was despised, and we held him of no account. Surely he has borne our infirmities and carried our diseases; yet we accounted him stricken, struck down by God, and afflicted. But he was wounded for our transgressions, crushed for our iniquities; upon him was the punishment that made us whole, and by his bruises we are healed.

ISAIAH 53:2–5

PRAYER

God who humbled yourself to share in our humanity through Jesus, help me to have a peaceful heart and a demeanor that demonstrates it. Make me an example of holiness at all times and in all circumstances. May I daily be more conformed to your will and keep my life in honest perspective. Let my every action and every moment be one seamless act of praise.

LENTEN ACTION

Most people in today's culture would not consider it healthy or holy to always be looking down at the ground. Certain things in Benedict's rule are more shaped by his own times. Nevertheless, the crux of this highest degree of humility is a sense of peacefulness conveyed by the humble person. He or she is not easily distracted and does not need to be constantly entertained or concerned with everyone else's business. When one reaches the greatest humility, it is not demonstrated in heroic acts or miraculous powers, but in simply being present to the ordinary in a new way. As this Lent draws to a close, pay attention to the ordinary things you do today. Have you grown in peacefulness this Lent? Are you being more realistic about your gifts and failings? Have others benefited from your day-to-day actions? Would anyone be able to see a change in you?

DAY 39

Love Casts Out Fear

*H*aving, therefore, ascended all these degrees of humility, they will presently arrive at that love of God, which being perfect, casts out fear. In virtue of this love all things which at first were observed not without fear, they will now begin to keep without any effort, and as it were, naturally by force of habit, no longer from the fear of hell, but from the love of Christ, from the very habit of good and the pleasure in virtue. May the Lord be pleased to manifest all this by His Holy Spirit in His laborer now cleansed from vice and sin.

RULE OF SAINT BENEDICT, 7:67–70

SCRIPTURE

Love has been perfected among us in this: that we may have boldness on the day of judgment, because as he is, so are we in this world. There is no fear in love, but perfect love casts out fear; for fear has to do with punishment, and whoever fears has not reached perfection in love. We love because he first loved us.

1 JOHN 4:17–19

PRAYER

All-loving God, help me always to want what you want. As Lent ends, I place my meager efforts before you, not in fear that I am inadequate but as a free expression of my love. Thank you for all you have given me. May I ever be motivated by gratitude and the joy of being loved.

LENTEN ACTION

No sooner has Benedict described how one should recognize sinfulness and fear judgment than he reminds the reader that fear is not the endpoint. Humility's ultimate realization is when one accepts life as it is, open to both success and failure in daily struggles, and eager for holiness at whatever cost. What things do you do merely from fear of disgrace or punishment or negative reactions from others? What things are hard for you, but you do them because someone who loves you expects it? Reflect on how love changes your attitude, your willingness, your perseverance. Remember that God loves you and wants you to be your best self even more than any human does.

DAY 40

Hail to the King

*B*ut Benedict desired to suffer the world's malice rather than receive its praises, rather to be worn out with labor for God's sake than flattered by worldly praise.

DIALOGUES II, I

SCRIPTURE

[A]fter throwing their cloaks on the colt, they set Jesus on it. As he rode along, people kept spreading their cloaks on the road. As he was now approaching the path down from the Mount of Olives, the whole multitude of the disciples began to praise God joyfully with a loud voice for all the deeds of power that they had seen, saying, "Blessed is the king who comes in the name of the Lord! Peace in heaven, and glory in the highest heaven!"

LUKE 19:35B–38

PRAYER

Hosanna to you, ruler of all the world. May I always sing your praise and faithfully follow you on your journey through suffering to glory. As I walk with you this Holy Week, give me a heart as humble as yours and help me to bring your peace to the world.

LENTEN ACTION

Only in the Gospel of Luke are there no palm branches. Rather, the people lay down their cloaks, one of the most necessary and valuable possessions of a poor person of that time. By contrast, ours is a culture of great abundance. Praise the king who comes in lowliness by giving some of your clothing or other assets to the poor so that you might lighten your load as you travel toward Jerusalem.

DAY 41

Caring for God's Beloved Ones

*T*heoprobus asked Benedict the cause of his tears]. The man of God answered, "All this monastery which I have built, and all that I have prepared for my brothers, have been handed over to the barbarians by the judgment of almighty God. Only with great difficulty have I been able to obtain that the lives of the monks should be spared. These words that Theoprobus heard, we have seen confirmed since we know how the monastery was destroyed by the Lombards. At night, when the monks were asleep, they broke in and plundered everything, but they could not take a single man. Thus almighty God fulfilled his promise to his faithful servant Benedict that even if all their goods were lost, their lives were protected.

DIALOGUES II, XVII

SCRIPTURE

While I was with them, I protected them in your name that you have given me. I guarded them, and not one of them was lost except the one destined to be lost, so that the Scripture might be fulfilled. But now I am coming to you, and I speak these things in the world so that they may have my joy made complete in themselves. I have given them your word, and the world has hated them because they do not belong to the world, just as I do not belong to the world. I am not asking you to take them out of the world, but I ask you to protect them from the evil one. They do not belong to the world, just as I do not belong to the world. Sanctify them in the truth; your word is truth. As you have sent me into the world, so I have sent them into the world.

JOHN 17:12–18

PRAYER

God our protector, you watch over all of your children and want them to be safe and happy. Yet many continue to be endangered by war and violence. Help me to be a peacemaker and a protector of every human life.

LENTEN ACTION

Even as he neared his own death, Jesus prayed for the lives of all whom he loved, and Benedict did the same. Neither was able to stop the violence that often overtakes innocent and good people, but they could offer their own virtuous lives in prayer and action on behalf of others. Do something that will show that you also wish that not a single soul be lost: the unborn, the victims of war or disaster, the starving, and the exploited.

DAY 42

TUESDAY OF PASSION WEEK

Love Your Enemies

*B*ut the venerable father, seeing that the priest's heart was so ardently set against his life, grieved more for him than for himself....When the priest watched Benedict's departure and rejoiced, the balcony on which he stood collapsed and crushed him, even though the rest of the house remained firm. Because the man of God had only gone ten miles away, his disciple Maurus decided to inform him, saying, "Come back because the priest who was persecuting you is dead." When Benedict heard this, he felt great grief and lamented both because his enemy had died, and also because his disciple had rejoiced.

DIALOGUES II, XVIII

SCRIPTURE

When those who were around him saw what was coming, they asked, "Lord, should we strike with the sword?" Then one of them struck the slave of the high priest and cut off his right ear. But Jesus said, "No more of this!" And he touched his ear and healed him.

LUKE 22:49–51

PRAYER

God of mercy, you gave us the example of perfect forgiveness in Jesus. Let me never rejoice in the sufferings of another and always forgive and love those who have wronged me. Bless those whose hearts are embittered by revenge and who inflict suffering on others, as well as those who are injured by them.

LENTEN ACTION

Everyone has rejoiced in someone else's misfortune at some time. If nothing else, we often comment on a news report or a story by saying, "Served her right," or, "That's what he gets." Try to think of such a time in your life. For whom have you not felt sorry? Whose injury does not bother you? Pray for those individuals or types of persons in a special way. Perhaps you might write a "letter" (you need not send it) in which you express your regret for your attitude.

DAY 43

Unspeakable Sweetness of Love

*B*ut even if, to correct vices or to preserve charity, sound reason dictates anything that turns out somewhat stringent, do not at once fly in dismay from the way of salvation, the beginning of which cannot but be narrow. But as we advance in the religious life and faith, we shall run the way of God's commandments with expanded hearts and unspeakable sweetness of love; so that never departing from His guidance and persevering in the monastery in His doctrine till death, we may by patience share in the sufferings of Christ, and be found worthy to be coheirs with Him of His kingdom.

RULE OF SAINT BENEDICT, PROLOGUE:46–50

SCRIPTURE

For all who are led by the Spirit of God are children of God. For you did not receive a spirit of slavery to fall back into fear, but you have received a spirit of adoption. When we cry, "Abba! Father!" it is that very Spirit bearing witness with our spirit that we are children of God, and if children, then heirs, heirs of God and joint heirs with Christ—if, in fact, we suffer with him so that we may also be glorified with him.

ROMANS 8:14–17

PRAYER

Not every day of this Lent has been easy, dear God, but I have tried to keep to the narrow way. Help me to accept my sufferings as Jesus did so that I might also come to eternal glory.

LENTEN ACTION

Discipline in Lent, or any other time, is not primarily about making life hard for no good reason. Rarely does anything come to us without hard work and sacrifice. Try to remember what it was like when you were first learning a particular skill or trying to change a habit. Replay in your mind how feeble your first efforts were, or how many mistakes and failures there were, or the times when you just wanted to give up. Now reflect on a time when you felt a great sense of achievement or enjoyment from that effort. If it is something you can still enjoy, do it today and thank God that you persevered through the narrow way.

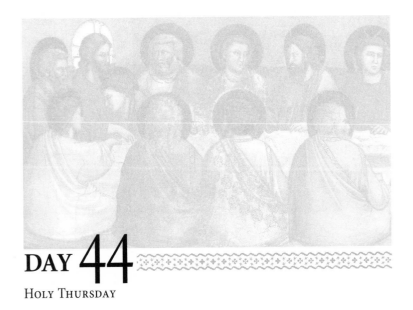

DAY 44

Washing One Another's Feet

*L*et the abbot pour the water on the guest's hands, and let both the abbot and the whole community wash the feet of all the guests. When they have been washed, let them say this verse: "We have received your mercy, O God, in the midst of your temple." Let the greatest care be taken, especially in the reception of the poor and travelers, because Christ is received more specially in them; whereas regard for the wealthy itself procures them respect.

RULE OF SAINT BENEDICT, 53:12–15

SCRIPTURE

And during supper Jesus, knowing that the Father had given all things into his hands, and that he had come from God and was going to God, got up from the table, took off his outer robe, and tied a towel around himself. Then he poured water into a basin and began to wash the disciples' feet and to wipe them with the towel that was tied around him....After he had washed their feet, had put on his robe, and had returned to the table, he said to them, "Do you know what I have done to you? You call me Teacher and Lord—and you are right, for that is what I am. So if I, your Lord and Teacher, have washed your feet, you also ought to wash one another's feet. For I have set you an example that you also should do as I have done to you.

JOHN 13:2B–5, 12–15

PRAYER

Servant God, you have shown us that we must be the least of all and at the service of all. Help me to humbly offer myself to others, not just those with whom I am comfortable, but especially to those who may feel unworthy or unvalued. Give them your loving touch through me.

LENTEN ACTION

Jesus made it clear by his actions that he was the servant of all, and willing to see himself as the lowliest of all, just as Benedict says about the truly humble and holy person. Serve someone today in imitation of Christ.

DAY 45

A Death That Brings Life

Scripture says: "He that shall persevere unto the end shall be saved." And again: "Let your heart take courage, and wait for the Lord." And showing that the faithful one ought even to bear every disagreeable thing for the Lord, it says in the person of the suffering: "For your sake we suffer death all the day long; we are counted as sheep for the slaughter."

RULE OF SAINT BENEDICT, 7:36B–37

SCRIPTURE

They made his grave with the wicked and his tomb with the rich, although he had done no violence, and there was no deceit in his mouth. Yet it was the will of the LORD to crush him with pain. When you make his life an offering for sin, he shall see his offspring, and shall prolong his days; through him the will of the LORD shall prosper. Out of his anguish he shall see light; he shall find satisfaction through his knowledge. The righteous one, my servant, shall make many righteous and he shall bear their iniquities. Therefore I will allot him a portion with the great, and he shall divide the spoil with the strong; because he poured out himself to death, and was numbered with the transgressors; yet he bore the sin of many, and made intercession for the transgressors.

ISAIAH 53: 9–12

PRAYER

You came to us as one of us and experienced the harshest of treatment. Help me to stand fast in suffering and boldly proclaim you as Lord and Savior. Give comfort to those who are harassed, imprisoned, or tortured because of their faith in you. Thank you for the great gift of yourself.

LENTEN ACTION

This day commemorates the brutal death of Jesus, which seemed to be his tragic end. Although we know that the story has a happy ending, we cannot skip over the suffering that he endured and the devastation and disillusionment his friends and family must have felt. Stand at the foot of the cross by spending some time in prayer before a crucifix or other image of the suffering Christ.

DAY 46

Raising the Dead

A peasant carrying his dead child came] crying: "Give me my son, give me my son!" The man of God, amazed at these words, stood still, and said: "Have I taken away your son?" To which the man replied, "He is dead: come and revive him." [Benedict replied] "Why will you lay such an unbearable burden on me?" But the poor man, urged on by his grief, persisted, swearing not to leave until his son was raised from death....The man of God came with his monks, knelt, and placed himself over the body of the little child. Raising his hands towards heaven, he said: "Lord, do not regard my sins, but the faith of this man who desires to have his son raised to life, and return to this body the soul which you have taken away." Scarcely had he finished the prayer when the soul returned and the child's body began to shudder. To the eyes of everyone present, it appeared that he was convulsed as by a miraculous jolt. Then he took the boy by the hand and gave him to his father, alive and well.

DIALOGUES II, XXXII

SCRIPTURE

Martha said to Jesus, "Lord, if you had been here, my brother would not have died. But even now I know that God will give you whatever you ask of him."...then Jesus, again greatly disturbed, came to the tomb. It was a cave, and a stone was lying against it. Jesus said, "Take away the stone."...The dead man came out, his hands and feet bound with strips of cloth, and his face wrapped in a cloth. Jesus said to them, "Unbind him, and let him go." Many of the Jews therefore, who had come with Mary and had seen what Jesus did, believed in him.

JOHN 11:21–22, 38–39A, 44–45

PRAYER

God of life, I believe with all my heart that Jesus is the Messiah, who brings eternal life. Raise me above the death that comes from sin and fear. Bless all who will die today, especially those with no one to grieve their passing. May their souls, and the souls of all the faithful departed, rest in peace.

LENTEN ACTION

Holy Saturday is the day in Holy Week on which nothing seems to happen. It is a day when Jesus' friends grieved because they thought he was gone forever. While we probably won't be able to see someone return from death, no one is gone forever when he lives in the loving memory of others. Raise some dead loved ones today by remembering them with affection. Look at pictures, visit their graves, do something to honor their memory.

PART II

~~~~~~~~

READINGS *for* EASTER

DAY 47

EASTER SUNDAY

Alleluia

While Benedict was dwelling as a hermit, the Lord appeared to a priest who was preparing his Easter dinner.] He said: "You have prepared delicacies for yourself, while my servant in such and such a place is afflicted with hunger pangs." Hearing this, the priest rose up on Easter day and went with the food he had prepared to seek the man of God amid the steep hills and low valleys and hollow ditches, and finally found him in his cave. They prayed together, blessed almighty God, and after spiritual conversation, the priest said: "Get up brother, and let us dine, because today is Easter." The man of God answered, "I know that it is Easter because I have had the honor of seeing you." For he had been away from human society for so long that he did not know it was the Solemnity of Easter. But the venerable priest insisted: "Really, today is the feast of our Lord's Resurrection and it is not right for you to fast. That is why I have been sent, so that we might eat together of almighty God's gifts." So, blessing God, they ate their meal.

DIALOGUES II, I

SCRIPTURE

But on the first day of the week, at early dawn, they came to the tomb, taking the spices that they had prepared. They found the stone rolled away from the tomb, but when they went in, they did not find the body. While they were perplexed about this, suddenly two men in dazzling clothes stood beside them. The women were terrified and bowed their faces to the ground, but the men said to them, "Why do you look for the living among the dead? He is not here, but has risen.

LUKE 24:1–5

PRAYER

Alleluia, praise to you Lord, on this glorious day of Easter. Thank you for this most wondrous gift to us. May I always hold to your words and proclaim you to the world.

EASTER ACTION

This is the day the Lord has made, a day for great rejoicing. Celebrate wholeheartedly by attending worship, feasting, and enjoying the company of others.

DAY 48

MONDAY OF EASTER WEEK

Companion on the Road

*T*hose who are at work too far away, and cannot come to the oratory at the appointed time (and the abbot has assured himself that such is the case), let them perform the Work of God in the fear of God and on bended knees where they are working. In like manner let those who are sent on a journey not permit the appointed hours to pass by; but let them say the office by themselves as best they can and not neglect to fulfill the obligation of divine service.

RULE OF SAINT BENEDICT, 50:1–4

SCRIPTURE

As they came near the village to which they were going, he walked ahead as if he were going on. But they urged him strongly, saying, "Stay with us, because it is almost evening and the day is now nearly over." So he went in to stay with them. When he was at the table with them, he took bread, blessed and broke it, and gave it to them. Then their eyes were opened, and they recognized him; and he vanished from their sight. They said to each other, "Were not our hearts burning within us while he was talking to us on the road, while he was opening the Scriptures to us?

LUKE 24:28–32

PRAYER

Companion on the journey, you walk with us every step of our lives, but we seldom recognize you. May my heart burn within me when I hear the sacred Scriptures and when you speak to me in my prayers.

EASTER ACTION

There is a custom in many places that the Monday of Easter week is celebrated by an "Emmaus walk," a special visit to some person or sacred place. This can be a reminder that Jesus joins us on all our journeys and also that Jesus wants us to carry the good news of his resurrection as well. Visit someone today and be a Christ-bearer. If you can't make an Emmaus journey, at least call or correspond in some way.

DAY 49

A Woman's Love

*T*herefore, by this [miracle of the storm for which Scholastica prayed] we see that he wanted something but was not able to have it. For if we know this venerable man's mind, there is no doubt that he would have wanted the same fair weather to continue as when he left his monastery. Instead of what he wanted, by the power of almighty God, he found a miracle brought about by a woman's prayers. Is it not a marvel that a woman who wished to visit with her brother longer, was able to be more effective than he was? She realized, as Saint John says, "God is love." Therefore, it is right that she who loved more was able to do more.

DIALOGUES II, XXXIII

SCRIPTURE

When she had said this, she turned around and saw Jesus standing there, but she did not know that it was Jesus. Jesus said to her, "Woman, why are you weeping? Whom are you looking for?" Supposing him to be the gardener, she said to him, "Sir, if you have carried him away, tell me where you have laid him, and I will take him away." Jesus said to her, "Mary!" She turned and said to him in Hebrew, "Rabbouni!" (which means Teacher). Jesus said to her, "Do not hold on to me, because I have not yet ascended to the Father. But go to my brothers and say to them, "I am ascending to my Father and your Father, to my God and your God.' "Mary Magdalene went and announced to the disciples, "I have seen the Lord"; and she told them that he had said these things to her.

JOHN 20:14–18

PRAYER

God of love, you blessed Mary Magdalene for her faith and counted her among your closest companions. Bless all women, especially those who are abused and those who are rejected as inferior by men and by cultural traditions. Fill me with the ardent love that filled the women who stood by Jesus at his death and rejoiced at his resurrection.

EASTER ACTION

Jesus was radical in his interactions with women. His mother Mary, Mary Magdalene, and countless holy women have been filled with the love of Christ. Do something special for a woman who loves you and also support oppressed or exploited women by engaging in some study, donation, or expression of concern.

DAY 50

Breaking Bread

*L*et them serve each other so that no one be excused from the work in the kitchen, except on account of sickness or more necessary work, because greater merit and more charity is thereby acquired.

RULE OF SAINT BENEDICT, 35:1–2

SCRIPTURE

He said to them, "Why are you frightened, and why do doubts arise in your hearts? Look at my hands and my feet; see that it is I myself. Touch me and see; for a ghost does not have flesh and bones as you see that I have." And when he had said this, he showed them his hands and his feet. While in their joy they were disbelieving and still wondering, he said to them, "Have you anything here to eat?" They gave him a piece of broiled fish, and he took it and ate in their presence.

LUKE 24:38–43

PRAYER

Provider God, your gift of food is more than just physical nourishment. Help me always to be grateful for what I eat, those with whom I eat it, and the work of all who produce it. Bless all the hungry of the world with help and hope. May I recognize you in the breaking of bread at both altar and table.

EASTER ACTION

The disciples recognized Jesus because of the many ways in which he had fed them, and by the special bond they had in eating together. Pay attention to how you eat. Do your meals resemble the holy feast of the Eucharist and the heavenly banquet? How can you eat in a more sacred manner and with greater appreciation?

DAY 51

Doubting Thomas

GREGORY: Why do you doubt, Peter, when you examine how this was done? It is clear that the soul is of a more mobile nature than the body....If Habakkuk, in his body, could travel so far in an instant, and carry dinner, what wonder is it that it was granted Father Benedict to go in spirit to tell the spirits of his sleeping brothers the necessary information? As Habakkuk traveled physically to bring physical food, so Benedict went spiritually to build up the spiritual life.

PETER: I confess that your words have satisfied my doubtful mind.

DIALOGUES II, XXII

SCRIPTURE

But Thomas (who was called the Twin), one of the twelve, was not with them when Jesus came. So the other disciples told him, "We have seen the Lord." But he said to them, "Unless I see the mark of the nails in his hands, and put my finger in the mark of the nails and my hand in his side, I will not believe." A week later his disciples were again in the house, and Thomas was with them. Although the doors were shut, Jesus came and stood among them and said, "Peace be with you." Then he said to Thomas, "Put your finger here and see my hands. Reach out your hand and put it in my side. Do not doubt but believe." Thomas answered him, "My Lord and my God!" Jesus said to him, "Have you believed because you have seen me? Blessed are those who have not seen and yet have come to believe."

JOHN 20:24–29

PRAYER

My Lord and my God, without seeing you I believe. Sustain me in times of doubt and keep my faith strong. Let me touch your wounds in the wounds of suffering people I encounter. Help me to know that truly you are present in them and that you want me to reach out and touch you.

EASTER ACTION

We all have our moments of doubt about our faith and whether Christ is truly with us. Use Thomas's prayer as a mantra today. Throughout the day, in quiet moments, or while waiting or walking or working, say in your heart, "My Lord and my God."

DAY 52

The Waters of Life

*M*aurus asked his father's blessing and obeyed his command, running to the place to which the current had carried the boy. Thinking he was still on land, Maurus ran on the water, grabbed Placid by his hair, and ran back with him. As soon as he was on land, he came to himself and looked back. Realizing that he had run on the water, he was amazed and shaken that he had done what he could never have dared to do. When he came back to Benedict and told him what had happened, the venerable man did not attribute this to his own merits, but to the obedience of Maurus.

DIALOGUES II, VII

SCRIPTURE

Just after daybreak, Jesus stood on the beach; but the disciples did not know that it was Jesus. Jesus said to them, "Children, you have no fish, have you?" They answered him, "No." He said to them, "Cast the net to the right side of the boat, and you will find some." So they cast it, and now they were not able to haul it in because there were so many fish. That disciple whom Jesus loved said to Peter, "It is the Lord!" When Simon Peter heard that it was the Lord, he put on some clothes, for he was naked, and jumped into the lake. But the other disciples came in the boat, dragging the net full of fish, for they were not far from the land, only about a hundred yards off. When they had gone ashore, they saw a charcoal fire there, with fish on it, and bread.

JOHN 21:4–9

PRAYER

Thank you, God, for the gift of water that gives us life. Thank you, too, for the saving waters of baptism by which we are cleansed and made holy. Help me to dive bravely into the springs of salvation that flow from you and be immersed in your love.

EASTER ACTION

Both before and after the resurrection, Jesus and his disciples experienced many wonders on and around water. At Easter, we celebrate the waters of our saving baptism and eternal life. Pay attention to water today. Use it reverently and briefly renew your baptismal commitment when you touch it.

DAY 53

SATURDAY OF EASTER WEEK

Gone Yet Present

*T*he one who is Truth, to increase the faith of his
disciples, said: "If I do not depart, the Paraclete will not
come to you." Since it is certain the comforting Spirit always
proceeds from the Father and the Son, why does the Son say
that he will depart so the Spirit, which never leaves the Son,
may come? Because the disciples, who beheld our Lord in
the flesh, always wanted to see him with their bodily eyes,
rightly did he say to them: "Unless I go away, the Comforter
will not come." It was as if he had plainly told them, "If I do
not go away, I cannot show you the love of the spirit. Unless
you cease to see me bodily, you will never love me spiritually.

DIALOGUES II, XXXVIII

SCRIPTURE

Nevertheless I tell you the truth: it is to your advantage that I go away, for if I do not go away, the Advocate will not come to you; but if I go, I will send him to you. And when he comes, he will prove the world wrong about sin and righteousness and judgment: about sin, because they do not believe in me; about righteousness, because I am going to the Father and you will see me no longer; about judgment, because the ruler of this world has been condemned. "I still have many things to say to you, but you cannot bear them now. When the Spirit of truth comes, he will guide you into all the truth; for he will not speak on his own, but will speak whatever he hears, and he will declare to you the things that are to come.

JOHN 16:7–13

PRAYER

Spirit of love, come to me anew and make your dwelling in my heart. May I believe ever more fervently in the word of Jesus and, strengthened by your gifts, grow in faith, hope, and love.

EASTER ACTION

Traditionally, the sevenfold gifts of the spirit have been enumerated as: wisdom, understanding, counsel (right judgment), fortitude, knowledge, piety, and fear of the Lord (awe and wonder). Of which are you most in need right now? Reflect on what the gift means in your current situations and pray especially for it.

DAY 54

SECOND SUNDAY OF EASTER

Zeal for God

*A*s there is a harsh and evil zeal, which separates from God and leads to hell, so there is a virtuous zeal which separates from vice and leads to God and life everlasting.... Let them prefer nothing whatever to Christ, and may He lead us all together to life everlasting.

RULE OF SAINT BENEDICT, 72:1–2, 11–12

SCRIPTURE

When the day of Pentecost had come, they were all together in one place. And suddenly from heaven there came a sound like the rush of a violent wind, and it filled the entire house where they were sitting. Divided tongues, as of fire, appeared among them, and a tongue rested on each of them. All of them were filled with the Holy Spirit and began to speak in other languages, as the Spirit gave them ability.... "You that are Israelites, listen to what I have to say: Jesus of Nazareth, a man attested to you by God with deeds of power, wonders, and signs that God did through him among you, as you yourselves know—this man, handed over to you according to the definite plan and foreknowledge of God, you crucified and killed by the hands of those outside the law. But God raised him up, having freed him from death, because it was impossible for him to be held in its power."

ACTS 2:1–4, 22–24

PRAYER

Almighty God, Savior Jesus, Spirit of Life, pour forth upon the earth and renew it by your power and grace. Inspire me to always feel your presence, love you, and proclaim you to the world. Send your mighty winds to all the places where people are still in the darkness of hatred, war, and oppression. Give me great zeal for you in all that I do, and keep me fervent in my journey toward my eternal home with you.

EASTER ACTION

Evangelist preachers are always exhorting people to "feel the power!" Can you feel the power of Jesus coursing through you? Pray for that sensation of being more than yourself, of being an instrument through which God sounds forth. Sit quietly, become aware of your own body, especially your breathing, and imagine light and power filling and energizing you. Then go out to the world and proclaim the good news in some way by your words or deeds. Jesus is truly risen! Alleluia!